GROWING IN THE GOSPELS

The Kabbalah Explains How

Jesus of Nazareth Became Divine

A mystical way to understand Jesus' divinity

Michael Harvey Koplitz

Published by Michael H. Koplitz

ISBN-13: 9798645706937

Table of Contents

THE LARGE MARGINS ARE INTENTIONAL. THEY ARE FOR YOUR NOTES (ONLY AVAILABLE IN THE PAPERBACK EDITION)

Before you start reading

I have been using Ancient Bible Study Methods developed initially by the Sage Hillel to analyze Scripture for many years. I learned the Greek/Western method of Scripture analysis while attending Seminary. I found that the Greek/Western process did not explain many of the events in the New Testament. Using a Hebraic approach to a Hebraic document has been opening up a deeper understanding of the LORD's Bible. I have incorporated the culture of Jesus' day and His native language, Aramaic, to expand the analysis of biblical passages.

The LORD's Bible contains various depths of understanding. The Rabbis say that there are at least seventy depths of understanding to the Torah. Why? Because a person will hear the Torah read at least that many times in their lives. The synagogue reads the Torah through each year.

Pardis is a system developed in the Middle Ages to group these depths of understanding (Pardis was developed by Kabbalist Rabbis). They are the literal form of the Bible, followed by the allegorical meaning, then the Midrash meaning, and finally, the secret meaning.

The Kabbalah created mostly in Safed, Israel in the 16th century, led by Isaac Luria comes from the Zohar and other mystical writings. Christian Kabbalist has also been studying the Zohar to try to gain a deeper understanding of the Bible.

What is presented here is an understanding of Jesus of Nazareth using the Kabbalah and the Zohar while cross-referencing the Bible. When you read this presentation, take note that I am not saying that this is what I believe nor what you should believe. It is an academic presentation.

In Hebraic studies, anything can be debated as long as the premise of the discussion is biblical. What is presented is biblical. Some readers will have difficulty reading this presentation because of what the church has taught them. The debate is not about the church is incorrect. It is a presentation of looking at the life of Jesus of Nazareth using the Kabbalah as the backdrop. If you feel that you will get angered by such a presentation, then I advise you to stop reading right now.

Hebraic studies allow for the free expression of ideas. Remember that none of us have a pure answer to the theological questions of the world. This statement is true because of the numerous religious expressions that exist in the world. Christianity today has many expressions. Today they have labels like Methodists, Lutherans, Catholics, and many more. Also, we have a new label for some churches, the independent churches. These independent churches develop what they want their theological position to be.

So if you are still reading this book, then you are open to reading something extremely different then what the church professes as the understanding of Jesus of Nazareth.

One last statement is that I am NOT saying that this is my theological position. I am presenting a possibility that is worth contemplating. That is all. Now, if you are ready and have an open mind, please continue to the introduction.

Introduction

Trinity doctrine states that the Father, Son, and Holy Spirit are three in one. No matter which theologian speaks or writes about the Trinity, they have difficulty explaining it. The example of water is often used to explain Trinity, but it is heresy according to the church's trinity doctrine. Water can exist in solid, liquid, and gaseous states at the same time and in the same vessel. Whether it is solid, liquid, or gaseous, these three physical forms of water are composed of molecules of two hydrogen atoms and one oxygen atom. The Father, Son, and Holy Spirit are all forms of God and all equal in power and knowledge.

Then how can Jesus the Son not know when he will return as indicated in the Gospels? Also, how can Jesus say the words about being abandoned by God when he is God at the cross? The church does not have a good explanation for this. When pressured, the answer is that there are ways of God that no human can understand. That is a true statement. However, it is not an encompassing statement.

The Kabbalah was developed in the 16th century, mainly in Safed Israel. It is based on the Zohar and other mystical writings. Isaac Luria developed the Tree of Life. The understanding of the Tree of Life has been discussed among rabbis and Christian theologians for centuries. The Zohar was presented to the Pope in the 16th century.

Christian Kabbalists intended to get the Pope to acknowledge that the Zohar should be considered a sacred set of books because it discloses the secrets of the Universe.

Several Christian Kabbalists believe that the Godhead, consisting of the first three emanations of Ein Sof (the word used in the Kabbalah for God); Keter, Chochmah, and Binah. The Father is Keter. The Son is Chochmah. The Holy Spirit is Binah. They believe this because Kabbalists, as a whole, envision the three initial emanations of Ein Sof that cannot be reached by a human soul. Moses was the only person in history who reached the emanation of Chesed, which is the fourth emanation. Some Kabbalists believe that there is a quasi-emanation (called Da'at) that exists and is a combination of Keter, Chochmah, and Binah. The emanations of Ein Sof are called Sefirah.

Another Christian Kabbalist view is that Keter is the Father, Tiferet is the Son, and the Shekinah is the Holy Spirit. The Shekinah is not a Sefirah like Keter or Chochmah. The Shekinah is the female attributes of Ein Sof that were trapped here when creation occurred. The Shekinah took on the responsibilities of bridging the gap between the emanations and the physical world.

This presentation is that Jesus was a human being who was able to climb the Ladder of Ascent past Chesed, which placed him in the God-Head, thus "becoming" divine.

Kabbalah

"Kabbalah is the name applied to the whole range of Jewish mystical activity. While codes of Jewish law focus on what it is God wants from man, kabbalah tries to penetrate deeper, to God's essence itself."[1]

There are secrets that the LORD wanted for us to discover that are hidden in the Hebrew Scriptures, especially the Torah. Kabbalah could be viewed as the process of discovering and understanding the secrets. The way the narratives are told in the Hebrew Scriptures reveal

[1] Kabbalah: An Overview, accessed May 12, 2020, https://www.jewishvirtuallibrary.org/kabbalah-an-overview.

the secrets. The grammar, the words, and even the letters of Hebrew direct students of the Kabbalah to discover the secrets.

The main text of the Kabbalah is the Zohar. "The most famous work of kabbalah, the Zohar, was revealed to the Jewish world in the thirteenth century by Moses De Leon, who claimed that the book contained the mystical writings of the second-century Rabbi Simeon bar Yochai. Almost all modern Jewish academic scholars believe that De Leon himself authored the Zohar, although many Orthodox kabbalists continue to accept De Leon's attribution of it to Simeon bar Yochai. Indeed, Orthodox mystics are apt to see Bar Yochai not so much as the Zohar's author as the recorder of mystical traditions dating back to the time of Moses. The intensity with which Orthodox kabbalists hold this conviction was revealed to me once when I was arguing a point of Jewish law with an elderly religious scholar. He referred to a certain matter as being in the Torah, and when I asked him where, he said: "It's in the Zohar. Is that not the same as if it was in the Torah itself?"

The Zohar is written in Aramaic (the language of the Talmud) in the form of a commentary on the five books of the Torah. Whereas most commentaries interpret the Torah as a narrative and legal work, mystics are as likely to interpret it "as a system of symbols which reveal the secret laws of the universe and even the secrets of God" (Deborah Kerdeman and Lawrence Kushner, The Invisible Chariot, p. 90). To cite one example, Leviticus 26 records "a carrot and a stick" that God offers the

Jewish people. If they follow his decrees, He will reward them. But if they spurn them, God will "set His face" against the people: "I will discipline you sevenfold for your sins...." and "I will scatter you among the nations" (26:28, 33). At the chapter's conclusion, God says: "Yet, even then, when they are in the land of their enemies, I will not reject them or spurn them so as to destroy them, breaking My covenant with them, for I am the Lord, their God" (26:44)."[2]

An essential text is the Sefer of Formation. "Sefer Yetzirah (Hebrew: ספר יצירה Sēpher Yəṣîrâh, Book of Formation, or Book of Creation) is the title of the earliest extant book on Jewish mysticism, although some early

---

[2] IBID.

commentators treated it as a treatise on mathematical and linguistic theory as opposed to Kabbalah. Yetzirah is more literally translated as "Formation"; the word Briah is used for "Creation". The book is traditionally ascribed to the patriarch Abraham, although others attribute its writing to Rabbi Akiva. Modern scholars have not reached consensus on the question of its origins. According to Rabbi Saadia Gaon, the objective of the book's author was to convey in writing how the things of our Universe came into existence."[3]

In ancient days a man had to be well trained in Torah before he could begin to study the Zohar. Also, he had to

---

[3] "Sefer Yetzirah," Wikipedia (Wikimedia Foundation, May 4, 2020), https://en.wikipedia.org/wiki/Sefer_Yetzirah.

be at least thirty years old. To fully understand and interpret the Zohar, a student must be fully instructed in the Torah, Prophets, and other writings of the Hebrew Scriptures. The Zohar is very dense and its secrets are well hidden. However, the LORD wants us to discover the secrets.

Reincarnation

The theological position of this book is that the reincarnation of the soul occurs, thus allowing a Ruach to continue to spiritually learn about the LORD's creation. According to the Zohar, a human soul is composed of five parts.

Nephesh – flesh

Ruach – spirit

Neshamah – the spark of God/breath of Ein Sof

Chayya – the "life force" which communes with Ein Sof

Yechida – the oneness with Ein Sof, being bounded, the human soul's connection to the infinite God.

Reincarnation can be considered the return of the Ruach from Yesod to Malchut, a rebirth. The Ruachim are created in the Tree of Life. The Ruachim travels through the Sefirot until they reach Yesod. A soul has a male and female component. Thus, it could be said that a new soul coming to Yesod is two different Ruachim (Spirits).

The Ruachim are divided into male and female, and individually they make their way to Malchut to live as flesh and blood and having the five components of the soul. The concept of soul mates is that the male and female Ruachim search for their opposite. Sometimes that happens, and other times it does not.

While on Malchut, it is the responsibility of the Ruach to learn as much as possible about the LORD and how the Universe, especially spiritually, works. As the Ruach absorbs and understands more about the ways of Ein Sof, the Ruach is able to climb the Ladder of Ascent (which will be described later).

When the Nephesh dies, the Ruach ascends to Yesod. The Ruach can flow through the Tree of Life to the Seforah, which corresponds to the amount of spiritual learning that was gained while in Malchut. It is believed that the Ruach would return to Malchut to continue in its learning until it has learned all that is necessary for the Ruach to pass from the Lower Waters to the Upper Waters.

There is a difference of opinion on whether a human Ruach can ever reach the Upper Waters of the Tree of Life. This question will be addressed later. Until the Ruach reaches the Upper Waters, it will return to Malchut, thus being reincarnated.

An evil example of reincarnation is the Jewish belief that Adolf Hitler was the reincarnation of Haman from the Esther story, and the reincarnation of Balak from the Genesis story of the talking Donkey (Numbers 26). Balak wanted Israel destroyed. So did Haman and Hitler. There are many connections between these three men. Thus, the Kabbalah belief of reincarnation says that these three men were the reincarnation of the same Ruach.

This belief is difficult for people to understand because why would the LORD allow such evil to reincarnate? Where does an evil Ruach go after the death of the Nephesh is an interesting question. Most religions believe that the evil person would go to some type of Hell. A Buddhist view is that the spirit returns to Earth to learn from its previous life's mistakes and continues the cycle until it has learned beauty and peace and then can enter Nirvana.

This belief is not that different from the Kabbalahist view of reincarnation. The Ruach will continue in its cycle of returning to Malchut until it learns everything that it needs to learn. The Kabbalist view is that the person will be told what they need to learn before they return to Malchut.

It is believed that a child can remember parts of their previous life until the age of four years old. There are numerous examples of young children telling their parents about their previous lives. Eventually, they cannot recall their past lives. Life regression hypnosis has been able to allow a Ruach to go back in time and talk about their previous life experiences.

A sign of reincarnation is how fast children today learn mathematics. Not all children will be able to learn higher levels of math, but for many, they are able to conquer higher mathematics long before their parents did. For example, in the 1970s, Calculus was taught in College. In 2020 Calculus is being taught in the High School. How can children today absorb so much more? One possible answer is that they had the basic mathematic skills from a previous life. This implies that some knowledge of Malchut remains with the Ruach. The person is not usually able to say where they learned the information, but they do know it. Thus, reincarnation is the vehicle that allows for deeper learning.

The Tree of Life

The Tree of Life was created by Ari, Isaac Lauria. It is a diagrammatic way to show what the Book of Formation says about how the Universe was created. One way to interpret the events is that Ein Sof sent His light out into a void that He created within Himself. That light instantly created the Sefirot Keter, Chochma, and Binah. These three sefirot are referred to as the "god-head."

Keter is the transition emanation between Ein Sof and His creation. It is unknown what exactly occurs in this realm. Chochma is considered the second realm, and it contains the wisdom of Ein Sof. Binah is the foundation sefirot for the remaining seven. One could say that Binah is the blueprint.

There are many opinions on how the Tree of Life operates and what Ruach and angels reside in each. For the author's interpretation, in diagram form, from several sources on the Tree of Life goto https://sites.google.com/view/zoharandkabbalahcharts. You will find several charts and documents related to the Zohar at this site.

There are twenty-two spiritual pathways that connect the ten sefirot. These pathways connect to the twenty-two letters of the Hebrew alphabet. Each spiritual pathway is assigned a Hebrew letter. Each Hebrew letter has a spiritual force that it emanates.

Each Sefirah offers different attributes of Ein Sof. In addition, as one spiritually travels through the Sefirah, one gains spiritual knowledge of the Universe.

The Tree of Life is a complicated part of the Kabbalah, and if the reader is not familiar with it, it needs to be studied. Remember that there are various opinions on how it works and what the relationships are in it. The ten Sefirot are universal and cannot be exchanged. It is the way the Sefirot react to each other and spiritual forces that is a debatable topic. Therefore, do not be surprised when you learn one way to examine the Tree of Life only to discover a different way because you are reading a different Kabbalist's interpretation.

The Ladder of Ascent

This is a spiritual component that is necessary to understand before moving into the theology of how Jesus of Nazareth became divine. This spiritual concept is that spiritually each Ruach commences the ascent in the Sefirot Malchut. This is the physical realm that humans live in. Through learning, education, and prayer, a human can rise up the ladder. Consider the ladder learning of spirituality.

New learnings are based on previous learning. The Ladder of Ascent is a way to describe a person's travel learning the spiritual secrets of the Universe. The more one learns, the higher one ascends on the ladder. The ladder rungs can be described using the ten Sefirot of the Tree of Life.

The Kabbalah says that Moses was the only human to reach the Sefirot of Chesed. This is based on Moses' reception of the name of the LORD, the Tetragrammaton, YVHV (Adonai). Each Sefirah has the name of the LORD associated with it.

The Kabbalah belief is that a human Ruach can not pass from the Lower Waters to the Upper Waters. To pass through the barrier that separates the Tree of Life would make a human Ruach divine.

Jesus Ascends the Ladder of Ascent

Now that the spiritual components have been laid out, the theological position of this work is that Jesus was the first human Ruach to ascent the Ladder of Ascent past Chesed. When he passed through Chesed to Binah, he became a part of the god-head. In doing so, his human Ruach became a divine Ruach.

Jesus' human Ruach must have gone through several reincarnations before it was ready to make this historic spiritual journey. The number of times Jesus' Ruach needed to be reincarnated is not known. It is also possible that he ascended the Ladder of Ascent to reach Chesed by the time of his death.

Whether Jesus' Ruach went through one or more reincarnations, it was during his lifetime that he obtained the spiritual knowledge to move past Chesed. The bottom line is that since Jesus was the first to move into the godhead that if one learns from him, then it is possible to move past Chesed.

The Messiah gave us the secret to entering into the Kingdom of Heaven. He also gave us the secret to move past the Sefirah of Chesed and onto Binah. It is not known what happens to a Ruach after it passes through the curtain of the god-head. That part of the Tree of Life is unknown.

Jesus' resurrection from death is something that the Kabbalah believes happens to all Ruachim. Ruachim returns to Yesod upon the death of the Nephesh. A difference for Jesus is that his Ruach was able to manifest itself in the world before leaving.

Several women came to his tomb three days after his death because the custom was that one the third day one could offer their farewells. The women were stunned when Jesus was able to manifest himself like a teraphim angel. They were able to see and touch him. This was something that had never happened before and has not happened since. Therefore, it may be possible for a human Ruach to manifest in the same way after death if that Ruach was passed into the god-head.

In his life, Jesus obeyed what the LORD told him to do. His spirituality had reached a climax for a human Ruach. In the Garden of Gethsemane, Jesus prayed to the LORD to take away the final step of his spiritual advancement. The final advancement was to sacrifice his life to prove to his followers and us that his convictions on how to interpret the Hebrew Scriptures and implement them were true. Jesus walked his walk and talked his talked every day of his life.

When he accepted his fate that night in the Garden, his Ruach was about to pass through Chesed into the god-head reaching Binah. To recap Jesus' death on the cross was his final test from the LORD to see if he was spiritually ready to pass into the god-head. He passed the test, which was proven by his resurrection appearances. It is the post-resurrection appearances that matter most. These appearances were proof from the LORD that Jesus had passed into the god-head.

The understanding of the god-head in the Tree of Life is clouded because of the veil that exists between Binah and Chesed. Kabbalist Rabbis may have a glimpse of what is going on, but in a general statement, it is a mystery of that part of the Tree of Life.

Jesus became divine because he passed into the god-head. He opened the doors to his followers, telling them that they could do the same thing.

Biblical References

Jer. 31:31 ¶ "*ª*Behold, days are coming," declares the LORD, "when I will make a *ᵇ*new covenant with the house of Israel and with the house of Judah,

Jer. 31:32 not like the *ª*covenant which I made with their fathers in the day I *ᵇ*took them by the hand to bring them out of the land of Egypt, My *ᶜ*covenant which they broke, although I was a husband to them," declares the LORD.

Jer. 31:33 "But *ª*this is the covenant which I will make with the house of Israel after those days," declares the LORD, "*ᵇ*I will put My law within them and on their heart I will write it; and *ᶜ*I will be their God, and they shall be My people.

These verses are the critical biblical reference to this presentation. As noted earlier, Moses was only allowed to reach the Sefirah Chesed. When Moses was at Mount Sinai, he received the name YHVH, which corresponds to Chesed.

When the prophet Jeremiah said that the LORD was to create a new covenant with His people, He was referring to allowing human Ruachim to pass through the veil that was between Chesed and Binah. The new covenant was to allow human Ruachim to learn the secrets of the Universe through spiritual learning.

Matt. 27:51 *a*And behold, *b*the ¹veil of the Temple was torn in two from top to bottom; and *c*the earth shook and the rocks were split.

When Jesus died on the cross, the veil of the Temple was torn in two, thus symbolizing that the LORD allowed Jesus' Ruach to pass from Chesed into Binah. The torn veil also symbolizes the new covenant that the prophet Jeremiah spoke. The Ladder of Ascent did not terminate with Chesed but now extends into the god-head. Human Ruach access to Binah, Chochmah, and Keter is now possible.

Jesus paved the spiritual path for human Ruachim to reach the god-head. The Gospels explain how the LORD wants us to use the Torah, Prophets, and Writings in order to follow Jesus through the torn veil between Chesed and

Binah and to come into a new covenant, a spiritual covenant with the LORD.

Bibliography

n.d. *Kabbalah: An Overview.* Accessed May 12, 2020.
    https:/www.jewishvirtuallibrary.org/kabbalah-an-overview.

n.d. *Sefer Yetzirah.* Accessed May 12, 2020.
    https://en.wikipedia.org/wiki/Sefer_Yetzirah.

Made in United States
Troutdale, OR
04/28/2024

19506939R00030